The ARTS

PAINTING AND SCULPTURE

Jillian Powell

Wayland

The Arts

Architecture
Cinema
Dance
Design
Literature
Music
Painting and Sculpture
Photography
Theatre

Cover illustration: Monet painting in his boat, by Édouard Manet.

Series and Book Editor: Rosemary Ashley
Designer: David Armitage
Consultant: Christopher McHugh, artist and lecturer

First published in 1989 by
Wayland (Publishers) Limited
61 Western Road, Hove
East Sussex BN3 1JD, England

British Library Cataloguing in Publication Data
Powell, Jillian
  Painting and sculpture. – (The Arts).
  1. Visual arts, to 1980s – Critical studies
  I. Title   II. Series
  709

  ISBN 1–85210–345–0

Typeset by DP Press, Sevenoaks, England
Printed and bound in Italy by Sagdos

Contents

1 Images

Every day, we are surrounded by images: moving images on television, video and film; and still images like posters or paintings, shop-window dummies or sculptures in wood, bronze or stone. These images mirror the world around us, or perhaps the world as we would like it to be. They reflect our concerns – our hopes and wishes as well as our worries and fears. Some images may make us happy, while others may make us angry or sad. Images have had the power to do this since the earliest paintings and carvings were made some 40,000 years ago.

To Stone Age peoples, an image carved in stone or painted using a mixture of earth pigments and animal fat, possessed magical powers. The earliest recorded cave paintings are in caves at Lascaux in France and Altamira in Spain. They show techniques similar to those used by the Australian Aborigines in their paintings on tree bark and rock faces. The Aborigines believe that the power of images can bring the rains or make a better harvest. In the same way, prehistoric peoples believed that by painting images of the wild animals needed for food and clothing, they could bring about success in the hunt.

Bottom *Bull and Horses, Lascaux, France. Prehistoric paintings show that art and magic were closely linked. Artists exploited the shapes of cave walls, using flint and bone tools to engrave outlines into the soft white stone, before dabbing on pigments.*

The lively paintings of bison, mammoths and horses that we see on the walls at Lascaux and Altamira are magical symbols. But they are more than this. In their energetic use of line and bold earth colours, they tell us something about the artists who painted them by fiery torch or grease lamp in caves deep underground, all those years ago. As in music and dance, painting and sculpture are a means by which we can express ourselves. Through painted and carved images, our Stone Age ancestors expressed their instinct for survival, skill in the hunt, and belief in the powers of magic.

Later, the earliest Christians expressed their beliefs on the walls of underground burial chambers, where they were hidden from the authorities when the practice of Christianity was forbidden in the Roman Empire. Religious beliefs have inspired many forms of art, from paintings on walls or behind church altars (altarpieces) to sculptures of Buddhist and Hindu gods. Painting and sculpture have been used to make objects for religious ceremony and prayer, and also to convey the ideas and teachings of various religions.

In medieval times, when most people could neither read nor write, images carved in stone or made in coloured glass (stained glass) were used to teach stories from the Bible as well as to make a church or cathedral a more beautiful place to worship in. During the medieval period, the wealthy church authorities, aristocracy and trades guilds commissioned artists to make a painting or carving for their church or chapel. Artists at this time were not widely known by name, and were regarded simply as skilled artisans or craftsmen.

As trade in commodities such as wool and silk brought wealth to merchants, they too began to commission works of art, sometimes for a private chapel in church, sometimes for their homes. They wanted religious works, and also portraits. For, in the days before photography was invented, painting and sculpture were the only means of recording what things looked like – whether a person, a place or an event. Roman sculptors had carved images of famous emperors, and many Roman faces are recorded in stone. Indeed, painting and sculpture can tell us much about life in the past – what people, their costumes, and their homes looked like.

By commissioning an artist, the patron, whether a Roman patrician or a medieval merchant, could enrich his home and display his wealth and taste. Pictures might be painted directly onto the walls and ceilings using a technique called *fresco*, or onto a wood panel, and later

Above *In Classical Greece and Rome, copper and bronze were used for sculptures ranging in size from the huge, 30 m high Colossus, to this little statuette, which measures only 18.5 cm high. Fine folds of drapery are used to define the form and create a pleasing balanced shape.*

Right *Michelangelo painted these frescoes for Pope Paul III's chapel in the Vatican when he was in his seventies. They were his last paintings, and some scholars have seen this figure mourning St Peter's crucifixion as a self-portrait of the ageing artist.*

canvas stretched over a wooden frame, to be hung on the walls of private apartments. Sculptors carved 'in relief' on the surfaces of buildings or tombs, or created free-standing sculptures for particular settings.

By the fifteenth century, at the beginning of the Renaissance period (a time of rebirth in the arts and learning) artists were becoming known by name and began signing their works. The work they did was still largely controlled by patrons. For example, the great Renaissance master Michelangelo was engaged by Pope Julius II to paint frescoes covering the ceiling of the Sistine Chapel in Rome, when he would have much preferred to continue work on a grand scheme of sculpture for the Pope's tomb. Nevertheless, artists throughout the ages have produced works which they made for themselves. Rembrandt's self portraits, for example, were not commissioned, but allowed the artist to explore mood and feeling by studying his own face in the mirror.

Changes in society and the economy meant that by the nineteenth century, artists were becoming much freer to paint and sculpt what they wanted. Annual exhibitions in major cities gave artists the chance to show their works to a much wider audience. Patronage was changing, with the middle classes, newly rich from industry, beginning to buy works of art as once only the upper classes had been able to do.

Our own century has seen changes in patronage, away from the private individual and towards sponsorship of the arts by the nation, local authorities and large companies and corporations. Some painting and sculpture is now commissioned directly by museums or galleries. The artist still has to satisfy those who commission or pay for his or her work, but painters and sculptors are much freer in the materials they use, in what they want to say, and in the way they express themselves.

From the earliest cave paintings, art has been a mirror of the age which created it. For prehistoric peoples, the hunt, and survival, were all important. Our own century has seen more changes than ever before – the introduction of the motor car and aeroplane, space travel and atomic bombs, mass-production of objects and images, changes in fashion, morals and the environment. Reflecting this restless and changing world, twentieth-century painters and sculptors have experimented ceaselessly with ideas. Art no longer has to be beautiful; in fact artists have used their works to express ugliness, fear and madness. All kinds of materials, even junk, have been used. Ours is the age of the computer and mass communication, and we are surrounded by moving images. Art has adapted to this too, with artists acting out art (Performance Art) or making sculptures that move (Kinetic Art), and even using the human body itself (Body Art).

There are no fixed rules or standards for art any more, except for our own eyes. It is important for us to decide what we want from art. When you look through this book or visit an art gallery, try to decide what you like (or dislike) and why.

Below *A modern sculpture showing how sculptors today experiment with shape and form, using materials like steel and techniques of welding and assemblage. Here, sculptors Lucy Byatt and Avril Wilson have used light, fanciful shapes to suggest the hair, creating a lively outline in which spaces are as important as the solid forms.*

② How Painting and Sculpture Began

Prehistoric art

It was during the Palaeolithic or Old Stone Age, about 40,000 years ago, that humans first began to draw, paint and carve. These prehistoric artists used natural earth colours: red and yellow ochres (kinds of rust found in the earth) and black from carbon (soot or charcoal from burnt remains, or coal), possibly mixed with animal fat as the Aborigines have used it for bark painting. At Altamira and at Lascaux, artists also made use of the shape of the cave walls, so that a bison painted on the ceiling appears to be rounded or solid in form.

Prehistoric hunters, already using stone tools and weapons, also carved figures in the round, using stone and ivory, and cut or engraved animals of the hunt on their spears. Carved figures show that the artist was not concerned to portray the human form accurately. Instead, the proportions or features were exaggerated for magical purposes. It was during the Neolithic or New Stone Age, about 10,000 BC, that humans learnt the art of combining copper and tin to make bronze, so preparing the way for future developments in sculpture.

By 3000 BC, around the eastern end of the Mediterranean, civilization had begun to establish itself in three main areas: the Nile Valley (Egypt), between the Rivers Tigris and Euphrates (Mesopotamia), and on the islands and coasts of the Aegean Sea (Cyclades and Crete). In each of these areas the arts were developed as an important part of society, and forms of painting and sculpture have been found in their remains. The characters of these early civilizations and their arts differed, and they influenced the development of each other to differing extents.

Egyptian art

Survival was the chief preoccupation for prehistoric peoples. But the people of Ancient Egypt, whose civilization lasted from about 3000 to 30 BC, had the wealth and leisure to create objects which were ornamental, and not simply functional like tools and weapons. Egypt's well-protected geographical position, and the fertile valley of the River Nile, meant that stable farming communities could develop, and with this stability came the man-power and the will to create monumental architecture, as well as wall paintings, sculpture, jewellery and glassware. People began to think about humankind's place in the universe, and learned men or priests kept written records of Egypt's history, using hieroglyphics (a form of picture writing).

Above *The Mesopotamian culture flourished from about 3000 BC between the rivers Tigris and Euphrates (modern-day Iraq). Mesopotamian art includes lifesize statues in stone and copper, and finely-carved relief sculptures. Numerous statues and reliefs depict Gudea, governor of Lagash. Here he is shown holding a spurting vase, a symbol of life and fertility.*

Religious customs dominated life in ancient Egypt, and religion was the chief influence on art. The Egyptians believed in life after death, and many works of art were concerned with preparations for the afterlife, when the soul entered the kingdom of Osiris, ruler of the living and the dead. After death, the body was carefully embalmed and bandaged before being placed in its coffin within a tomb. Furniture, plants and seeds, musical instruments and statues of attendants, would then be placed in the tomb to provide for the dead person's needs in the afterlife.

Pictures and stories were painted on the tomb walls. The Egyptian artists followed strict conventions in the portrayal of the human figure, showing the head and legs in profile, the shoulders and eyes as if viewed from the front. In this way, the artist was able to give a more complete image of the person represented, an approach revived by Picasso in his Cubist works in the twentieth century.

Below *Corn storers and gleaner from the Tomb of Menna at Thebes in Egypt. Wall paintings in Egyptian tombs can tell us much about daily life in Ancient Egypt. This mural, painted about 1400 BC, follows the stages of a harvest, from servants measuring the field with a rope, to the cutting of the crop with sickles.*

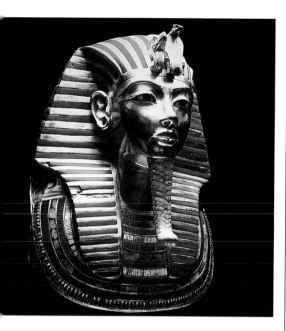

Above *Gold Mask of Tutankhamun, c.1350 BC. The Tutankhamun treasures, discovered in 1922, represent the only burial of an Egyptian Pharaoh found almost intact. This mask of solid gold, burnished and inlaid with precious metals, was placed over the head of Tutankhamun's mummy, outside the bandages in which the body was wrapped.*

Below *A Greek amphora showing the technique of red-figure vase painting, used in the fifth century BC. It allowed free and expressive designs, like this lively battle scene.*

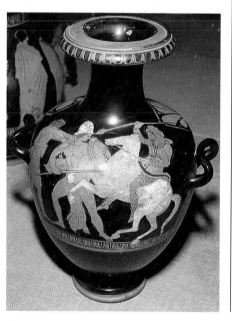

There were also strict conventions for sculptors, who were skilled at working in stone. Egyptian sculptures are characterized by their simple yet monumental form, calm balance and symmetry, and with both feet placed firmly on the ground. Early sculptures were carved from the front and the sides, making it possible to sense the solidity and stability of the stone blocks from which they were cut. The sculptors idealized their subjects, making their features regular, their expressions serene, and their poses dignified. This reflected the majesty of the Egyptian Kings or Pharaohs who, after death, became gods.

Classical art of Greece and Rome

It was during the seventh century BC that the Archaic (early) style of Greek art emerged. Adapting Egyptian techniques, sculptors carved free-standing figures of men (*kouroi*) and women (*korai*) for temple dedications. We recognize sculptures of this period by their serene, smiling expressions and rigid, symmetrical poses, with their hair carved in balanced curls and their garments falling in measured folds. Stone blocks were marked out precisely in sections before carving, and gradually techniques became more refined. Sculptors benefited from a more advanced knowledge of anatomy, and perfected techniques of casting in bronze.

Greek art reached its pinnacle during the fifth century BC, called the Classic Age, from which much Western culture and art is derived. Under the leadership of the statesmen Pericles, the Acropolis in Athens, destroyed by the Persians, was rebuilt. Leading craftsmen were employed to build and decorate the temples of the Acropolis, including the chief temple or *Parthenon*, which was dedicated to the goddess Athena. The sculptures, which filled the triangular temple ends or pediments and ran in relief along the temple friezes, show the features which characterize Greek art of the Classic Age. Figures are skilfully carved, showing the sculptor's mastery of anatomy and his lively sense of movement. He still idealizes his subjects, but the stiffness and simplification of Egyptian and Archaic art have now given way to a much more relaxed and sensitive understanding of the human form.

Greek painting is known to us mostly from surviving pottery. Clay pots were modelled in a variety of shapes and were used for many different purposes. They were decorated with scenes from mythology. Three main styles developed; firstly black figures on the natural reddish background of the clay, later black backgrounds leaving the figures in red, and finally shaded white figures usually on a white background. With the Roman conquest of Greece in 146 BC, many Greek works of art were plundered and brought back to Rome. Wealthy Roman patrons employed sculptors to copy their favourite Greek masterpieces, and today many Greek sculptures which were originally cast in bronze are now known only from Roman marble copies.

Roman painting, known to us chiefly from the wall paintings which have survived at Pompeii and Herculaneum, continued the free and lively style developed from the late Classical Greek period. In keeping with the greater realism of Roman sculpture, painters introduced more expression, made more attempt to represent space, and often used subjects from everyday life. Portraiture, especially, reached new heights of popularity and realism, both in sculpture and painting.

Below *A wall painting in the Villa of Mysteries at Pompeii. The paintings are believed to have been done by an artist in the first century BC and show a young woman being initiated into the rites of Dionysus, god of wine and revelry.*

③ The Art of Tribal Cultures

African negro art

Archaeological evidence indicates that Africa was the birthplace of the human race. Stone tools and rock paintings suggest that it was also the birthplace of art. The Negro culture has produced some of the most intense and imaginative art in the world.

The Negro people originated in West Africa, expanding southwards from the first century AD. Their art was inspired by a belief in the world of spirits and the desire to serve those spirits by offering statues or masks, with the aid of music, magic and ceremony. It was believed that once a man put on his masks and robes, he became the spirit he represented, which might be an ancestor, an animal, war or justice.

Similarly, African sculptors believed that the objects they made possessed a life force or soul. A figure, carved from wood or ivory, or cast in bronze, might embody the power of fire or an enemy. The forms themselves were simplified. Proportions and features were often exaggerated by the sculptor, who was trying to make visible the essential spirit within.

Above *A Guru mask from the Ivory Coast. African tribal masks were of various types and were used in many tribal ceremonies. Often, they were made by the wearer, but sacred masks were carved, or forged by woodcarvers or blacksmiths who were also sorcerers. The masks are often highly decorative, showing a fine sense of texture in the contrast between carved lines, or 'reeding', and smoothly rounded forms.*

Left *Wooden carvings were widely used by African tribes for religious or ritualistic purposes. This funerary screen from Nigeria represents the witch-doctor or medicine man, Ngbula.*

12

Aboriginal art

Australia and the islands of the South Pacific were peopled by immigrants from the Asian mainland, from many different ethnic groups. The Aborigines were established all over the Australian continent by 4000 BC. They were a nomadic people, roaming in small groups in search of food and water. They developed a life with few possessions but one that was rich in myth and ceremony, and closely in tune with the land, animals, plants and weather.

Art was considered the gift of a supernatural power. The Aborigine was chiefly an outdoor artist, illustrating his beliefs in the origin of the world and the workings of nature, in paintings on rock faces or in sacred caves, and on shields, tree bark or the human body. The rock paintings were renewed every year to ensure that the rains would not fail, and magical values were also attributed to painted or carved decorations on objects such as spears, boomerangs and baskets.

Much Aboriginal art was abstract, consisting of spirals, circles or parallel lines, and each tribe attached its own significance to the various patterns, according to the mythology of the tribe. The artist represented ancestral beings, and life forms known as 'totems', from which his group traced its descent. Elaborate designs were carved on the most sacred objects, the *tjurunga* (circular or oval slabs of wood or stone) which were used by the elders of the tribe in initiation ceremonies.

The largest Aboriginal sculptures are grave posts commemorating dead warriors, which may be carved from hardwood with stone tools and decoratively painted. But one of the most unusual forms of Aboriginal art is bark painting, using red, brown and yellow ochre with white pipe clay and charcoal, mixed with animal blood and fats or fruit juice to adhere to the bark surface.

Above *These paintings are situated in caves at the foot of Ayers Rock in the Northern Territory, Australia. The caves are sacred to several Aboriginal tribes. Aboriginal paintings range from simple human or animal figures to abstract patterns. Although some are connected with Aboriginal mythology and ritual, others are purely decorative.*

13

Maori art

Centuries of isolation shaped the art of the Maori people of New Zealand. Art was found in every aspect of Maori life, from the growing of the sweet potato crop to warfare, ancestor worship, social status and death. Human and animal figures, including the popular *manaia* or bird man, were important motifs, and the Maori sculptor was skilled at working in wood, bone, and stone.

Art was also applied to the human body in the form of tattoos, elaborate hair ornaments and cloaks of flax, decorated with dog skins, fur and feathers. Costume reflected the status of chiefs and many personal possessions, such as food bowls, and the treasure boxes *waka huia*, in which chiefs stored their sacred hair ornaments, were objects of art. Decorative carving was applied to weapons and canoes, agricultural tools, and to burial posts and monuments connected with ancestor worship.

Left *Maori sculptors delighted in the intricate, spiralling patterns and high degree of surface finish shown on this Totem carving from Polynesia. Craftsmen and their tools were honoured because it was believed they were guided in their work by a god.*

Below *Totem poles were carved by the North American Indians with 'totems' or emblems, usually in the form of animals. They proclaimed the ancestry and status of wealthy chiefs. Each animal or spirit carved on the pole has a special meaning, and together they tell a story or myth relating to the tribe concerned.*

Pre-Columbian art

The cultures which flourished in Central America and along the Pacific coast of South America before the Spanish conquest in the sixteenth century, were agriculturally settled and skilled in the arts, leaving behind them the remains of massive monuments as well as sculpture, textiles and mosaic artefacts.

The Incas of Peru, famed for their mighty fortresses, were also skilled potters and weavers, producing a great variety of decoration, chiefly in intricate geometric designs. The Aztecs, who dominated the valley of Mexico from AD 1300, were fine sculptors, carving figures of gods and beasts and richly decorated masks and skulls, often overlaid with shell and precious stones. Like other Pre-Columbian civilizations, they believed that the end of the world could only be prevented by ritual human sacrifice, and the artefacts they produced include sacrificial knives.

North American Indian Art

The art of the native North American Indian embraces different styles and cultures, but broadly speaking, all are concerned with religious beliefs and daily life, celebrating hunting scenes as well as the power of natural or supernatural forces.

The Inuit (or Eskimo) culture produced a variety of carving in ivory and wood as well as festival masks, sealskin and woven bags. Using all the raw materials available to them – walrus ivory and bone, whale bone, sealskin, stone and driftwood – the Inuit developed an artistic vocabulary of human and animal forms and geometric patterns which they believed possessed magical values.

The north west coast tribes developed a highly expressive sculpture, often used to decorate totem poles, and to celebrate the abundance of nature. More recently, the Inuit of Northern Canada have begun producing stone carvings of everyday objects in slate, and these have become popular forms of 'ethnic' art in the twentieth century.

4 Islamic and Oriental Art

Islamic art

The Islamic empire was flourishing when Western Europe was in the Dark Ages. At its height, it extended from India in the east to West Africa and Spain in the west. As the empire expanded, the Arabian peoples absorbed different cultures, and Islamic art reflects this. The Islamic faith was founded in the seventh century by the Arabian prophet Muhammad. Islamic beliefs, set down in the Qur'an, forbade artists to represent living things realistically, but elaborate designs were created using geometric devices and animal, vegetable and floral motifs. Sculptors were not allowed to work in the round, but were restricted to relief carving. They created ornate patterns of flat, often symmetrical designs, incorporating scrolls and twining leaves. The same intricate designs are characteristic of the world-famed Persian carpets, and of Persian and Indian manuscript illustration of the sixteenth century. Scenes of war, the hunt and court life were depicted in decorative designs characterized by their flowing lines and lettering and skilful interweaving of human and animal forms.

Above *This manuscript illustration shows the brilliant, jewel-like colours and decorative design characteristic of the Persian school of painting from the fifteenth to the seventeenth century. The painter has arranged shapes and colours in a flat pattern rather than representing space realistically, and has embellished his design with fine detail. The flowers, rocks, flags, even the blood from the fallen soldier, are painted decoratively rather than realistically.*

Indian art

India was the birthplace of many oriental art styles just as Greece was the birthplace of western art. Indian painting and sculpture are rooted in philosophy, and in the Hindu and Buddhist religions. The Indian artist does not represent objects from nature, or idealize them as the Greeks did. He is not concerned with the outward appearance of objects, but rather with the ideas they express, and with the feelings they arouse in the spectator. Works of art are the result of long contemplation of objects, often using the methods of yoga and meditation. The artist then works from his mental image, or inner vision.

The major art form of India is sculpture, illustrating the lives and powers of the Hindu gods, Brahma, Vishnu and Shiva, represented in various human and animal forms. Hindu shrines are decorated with ornate relief carvings, while those of the Buddhist faith are relatively simple. It was not until the second century AD that images of Buddha appeared in human form, and it was during the Gupta dynasty, from the fourth to the sixth century, that Buddha acquired his characteristic serene, spiritual image. It was from India that the Buddhist faith spread to China, Japan and elsewhere, and the graphic, linear qualities of Chinese painting during the T'ang dynasty can be traced back to Indian painting of the Gupta period.

Right *Krishna playing the flute in a grove, attended by a chauri-bearer. The legend of the Hindu god Krishna inspired many paintings and miniatures such as this manuscript illustration of the Basohli School, dating from about 1710. The colours are characteristically brilliant, and the faces stylized, shown in profile with large, intense eyes.*

Right *One of over 2,000 lifesize terracotta warriors and horses found near Mount Li in western China, in the burial mound of the Emperor Shih-Huang-Ti, first ruler of the Ch'in dynasty (221–206 BC).*

Below *Avalokitesvara embodies the wisdom and compassion of the Buddha and is shown here welcoming the souls of the dead. The statue, carved in Japan in the fourteenth century, is made from lacquered and gilt wood, elaborately decorated with gilt bronze, crystal and stones.*

Chinese art

The two religious creeds in China of Taoism and Buddhism (the latter introduced from India in the first century AD), and the philosophy of Confucius, have shaped Chinese art. To the Chinese artist, the work of art is a springboard to the world of the spirit, enabling the spectator to reach a state of ecstasy through the contemplation of purity. Chinese art is rooted in tradition. The Chinese worshipped their ancestors and revered the past, and many of their works of art are re-workings of traditional themes and ideas. Before the Buddhist religion became established, towards the end of the fifth century, three-dimensional sculpture consisted of figures placed in tombs to accompany the dead, and ritual vessels which were used in religious rites. The arrival of Buddhism gave rise to a demand for larger sculptures in the round.

It was during the T'ang period, from the seventh to the tenth century, that Chinese painting was at its height. Chinese painters were usually also philosophers and poets and their landscapes express a poetic contemplation of nature. Rather than recording the scene before them, Chinese painters select certain characteristic features from the landscape, and arrange them across the picture surface without regard for the rules of Western perspective. Fine brushstrokes are used for motifs such as trees and mountains, with fluid washes of thin colour overlaid to suggest space and atmosphere.

Japanese art

Like Chinese art, Japanese art developed indirectly from Indian Buddhism. Teachers and artists travelled from China to the Japanese islands from the eighth century, introducing religion and art. Early Japanese painting and sculpture echoes contemporary Chinese styles, although Japanese sculptors relied on wood or bronze because they had very little stone. A new, less formal and more realistic style developed during the rule of the Minamoto, a military family who came to power in 1185, establishing their court at Kamakura. Later, the new realism is especially marked in the coloured woodblock prints produced from the seventeenth to the nineteenth century.

Among the most famous woodblock artists were Kitagawa Utamaro (1753–1806) and Katsushika Hokusai (1760–1849). Many of these colourful woodblock prints found their way to Europe in the nineteenth century, and when they were first seen in Paris in the 1860s, they had a profound influence on the young artists who became known as the Impressionists and Post-Impressionists. These artists were inspired by the large, flat areas of colour, decorative lines and strong sense of design of the woodblock prints.

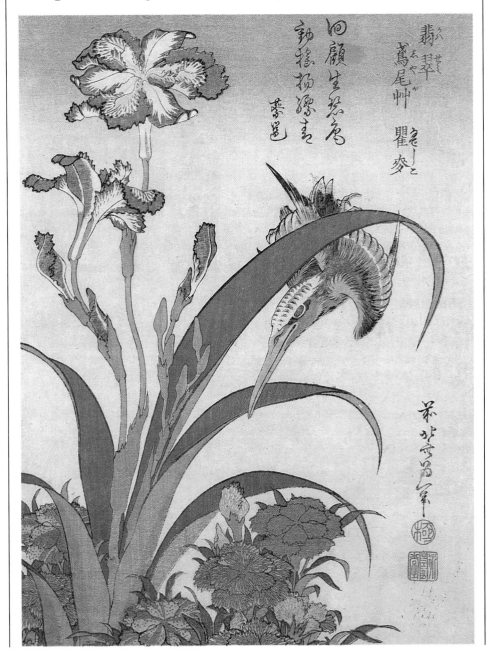

Left Irises, Pinks and Kingfisher, *painted by Katsushika Hokusai about 1830. Hokusai (1760–1849) was a master of the Japanese colour print. His bird and flower pieces, dating from the late 1820s, widened the range of subject matter available to the woodblock printer, and show his strong sense of colour and design.*

⑤ European Movements in Painting and Sculpture

The Roman Empire had dominated the Mediterranean for over 400 years when, in the fourth century AD, the capital was moved from Rome to Constantinople (previously called Byzantium, now Instanbul). From this date the Empire began to lose its control of Europe, and accepted the Christian religion. This was the beginning of the Byzantine culture in the East, and the Dark Ages in the West.

Byzantine art
The character of Byzantine art was formed by a mixture of Classical and Eastern traditions, and Christianity, which had spread through the Eastern Roman Empire and was beginning to expand into Europe. The Church disapproved of 'idols', so pictures became much more important than sculpture. The most striking remains of Byzantine pictorial art are the mosaics covering the inside walls of churches and the small devotional pictures known as 'icons'.

The Dark Ages in Europe were a period of great change and confusion, the only consistency being the gradual spread of Christianity. During this time the monasteries remained strongholds of learning and art. By the eleventh century churches were in great demand, creating a need for sculpture to adorn and enrich them.

Medieval art
The art of monumental sculpture known to the Greeks and Romans had died, so at first sculptors looked to illustrated manuscripts for their subject-matter and approach. During the eleventh and twelfth centuries, a distinctive style of architecture and sculpture emerged, known as 'Romanesque', from the round-headed or Roman arches that were being used. The most important sculpture of a church was usually to be found on the *tympanum*, or semi-circular area over the

Above *Icon of the Virgin Mary and Saints Theodorus and Georgius, with angels. It was painted in the sixth century and is now in St Catherine's Monastery, Sinai.*

Left *Detail of a page from the Luttrell Psalter (Book of Psalms) showing how medieval artists integrated text and illustrations. Seasonal tasks such as the ploughing shown here were popular illustrations for psalm and prayer books.*

main entrance. One of the finest such *tympana* is on the church of La Madeleine at Vézelay in France.

Free-standing sculptures were also carved in wood, sometimes covered with beaten gold and silver, and inlaid with precious stones, to serve as reliquaries (receptacles to contain the relic of a saint's body). Such reliquaries attracted pilgrims from far afield.

Towards the end of the Romanesque period, increased wealth from trade led to the growth of towns and the construction of universities and great cathedrals. Builders developed new methods of construction, which allowed them to use large windows to fill the nave with light. Stories from the Bible were depicted in glowing stained glass and in stone sculpture around doorways and column heads (known as capitals). Many decorated capitals represent the daily life of local people, and show great humanity and humour. This period, beginning in the twelfth century, is known as the Gothic period.

In Italy, the new style of Gothic art was partly inspired by the teaching of St Francis of Assisi. Artists like the Florentine Giotto (c1266–1337) carefully observed figures and landscape, showing a greater understanding of three-dimensional form and space as well as a more lively approach to story-telling. By the end of the fourteenth century, artists were travelling widely within Europe, and their exchange of ideas led to the emergence of a style known as International Gothic. Altarpieces such as the *Adoration* by Gentile da Fabriano (c1370–1427), painted in the early fifteenth century, show the rich detail, glowing colours and 'gilding', and decorative surface

Below The Adoration of the Magi *altarpiece by Gentile de Fabriano, painted in 1423.*

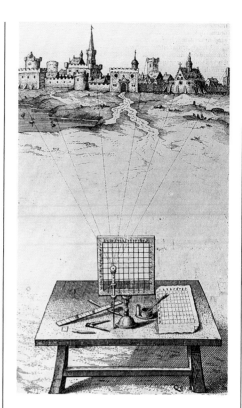

Above *A seventeenth-century illustration for a method of drawing a distant scene in perspective, using a perspective frame with a grid and viewer, combined with squared paper.*

Right St George and the Dragon *by Paolo Uccello, c.1460. In the National Gallery, London. Uccello was a pupil of the sculptor Ghiberti. Here he depicts a popular legend – citizens were regularly fed to the dragon, and when it was the turn of the King's daughter, St George came to her aid and wounded the creature. This is a rare picture for its time, in that it is painted on canvas, whereas most Italian pictures of the mid-fifteenth century are painted on wood panels.*

patterns which are characteristic of the style. Religious subjects continued to predominate during this period, but there was a growing interest in portrait painting, and a great demand for illustrated manuscripts, some depicting scenes from everyday life.

Renaissance art

The term Renaissance means re-birth, and describes the revival of Classical learning and art which began in Italy in the fifteenth century (or *Quattrocento*). While church authorities continued to commission painters and sculptors as they had done throughout the medieval period, a new class of patron emerged – wealthy merchants and bankers who had money to spend to enrich their homes and enhance their standing in society. The prosperous city of Florence became the centre of the new learning and art, and the powerful ruling Medici family gathered to their court some of the greatest artists, writers and philosophers of the day. Artists were in great demand, and now commanded more respect than they had done during the medieval period. They began signing their works, and it was during this period that individual artists first became known for their achievements.

The painter Masaccio, who lived from 1401–28, broke away from the elegant and decorative surface patterning of the International Gothic style, producing paintings which introduced a new naturalism in the representation of figures in space, and also in the portrayal of human emotions. Masaccio's paintings mark two important breakthroughs which were to shape Western art for centuries. Firstly, he applied the rules of scientific perspective, formulated by the Florentine architect Brunelleschi (1377–1446), to give an illusion of depth in his paintings. Secondly, he used light and shade or *chiaroscuro*,

Left *Ghiberti's bronze relief Baptistry doors at Florence, depicting David and Goliath. Ghiberti won the competition to design the new doors for the Baptistry in Florence in 1401. His bronze reliefs exhibit brilliant workmanship, with varying depth of modelling used to suggest space, and a graceful use of line and pattern.*

Below *Donatello's bronze statue of* David, *c.1440–42. It is in the Museo Nazionale in Florence.*

to make his figures appear to have volume or rounded form. The illusion of figures occupying space was made more convincing still by his use of colours, using greyer and 'cooler' colours for objects further away from the viewer.

The excitement experienced by the *Quattrocento* artists in representing space is evident in the works of Paolo Uccello (1397–1475). His paintings combined the laws of perspective with the lively sense of pattern characteristic of medieval art.

Sculptors, too, began using the new awareness of perspective and light and shade to give their works a more convincing illusion of reality. The bronze doors created by the Florentine sculptor Lorenzo Ghiberti (1378–1455) for the baptistry in Florence illustrate scenes from the Bible in a series of reliefs which are skilfully modelled to suggest figures receding in space. The great Renaissance master Michelangelo, on seeing Ghiberti's doors for the first time, said that they were 'so fine they might fittingly stand at the gates of paradise.'

Like Renaissance painters, sculptors of the period were inspired not only by contemporary thought and discovery, but by the art of Classical Antiquity. Donatello (1386–1466) had studied Classical art in Rome, and his bronze statue of *David* was the first free-standing, life-size statue since Classical times. Slender and graceful, *David* shows the Classical device of *contrapposto*, with his weight on one leg and his torso turned to give a sense of movement and vitality. The sinuous quality of line shown by Donatello's *David* is also found in the

Above Botticelli's Birth of Venus, *c.1484–86, in the Uffizi Gallery, Florence. According to legend, Venus was born from the sea foam and blown by the west wind onto the shores of Cyprus.*

works of the Florentine painter Sandro Botticelli (c1444–1510) whose playful mythological scenes sometimes disguise religious meaning. Botticelli's paintings show the pale, fresh quality of his medium – tempera, but by the mid-fifteenth century, the new technique of painting with oils had been introduced to Italy from the North, where it was first perfected by the van Eyck brothers working in Flanders. Trading links encouraged the exchange of ideas between Italy and the North, and the German painter Albrecht Dürer (1471–1528) was the first to introduce Renaissance ideas about perspective and scientific observation to Northern Europe. Dürer, who had trained in painting, engraving and woodcut printing, travelled to Italy as a young man and was influenced by the works he saw there, as was the Swiss-born painter Hans Holbein (c1497–1543). Holbein introduced Renaissance ideas to England when he came to work for the court of Henry VIII, and his portraits show Italian influence in their careful observation, balanced compositions and sense of dignity.

These qualities reached their peak in the works of the High Renaissance masters. Leonardo da Vinci (1452–1519) was the Renaissance ideal of the 'universal man', showing skill in many fields, from anatomy and astronomy to architecture and defence. His paintings show his mastery of the rules of perspective, and of conveying human emotion and drama. In the *Last Supper* fresco, painted for the monastery of Santa Maria delle Grazie in Milan, all lines of perspective lead to the central figure of Christ, a serene presence in a scene of tension and drama. Leonardo also developed a technique called *sfumato*, in which he blended different shades of paint to soften outlines, and suggest misty distances bathed in light and atmosphere. His paintings, whether religious groups of the Madonna and Child, or portraits such as the *Mona Lisa*, are always skilfully composed, using the shape of a triangle to achieve calm and stability.

Right *Leonardo da Vinci's* Mona Lisa *(La Gioconda), painted in 1503, now in the Musée de Louvre, Paris. Mona Lisa was the wife of the Florentine Marquese del Giocondo. This portrait shows Leonardo's device of* sfumato *in the misty landscape and rather mysterious figure, which has made it one of the most famous images in the history of art.*

Far left *Dürer's self-portrait, painted in 1498, at the Prado, Madrid. Dürer drew his first self-portrait at age thirteen. In 1494 he travelled to Italy, and this portrait, painted when he was twenty-six, shows him as a well-travelled and elegantly-dressed young man.*

The same sense of order can be found in the works of Raphael Sanzio (1483–1520) who was born in Urbino. One of Raphael's most important commissions was to decorate the papal rooms in the Vatican Palace in Rome with frescoes. One of the most famous, *The School of Athens*, represents the Greek philosophers Aristotle and Plato with their followers. It displays all the ideals of the High Renaissance, such as a balanced, orderly composition, a convincing illusion of forms and figures in space, and a celebration of man's role within the universe.

These ideals were spectacularly realized in the works of Michelangelo Buonarotti, (1475–1564) the sculptor, painter and architect, whose skills earned him the nickname 'the divine Michelangelo'. Michelangelo studied Classical sculpture in Rome, and established his reputation with monumental works carved from stone, such as the *Pietà* in St Peter's, Rome, and the colossal *David*, which was commissioned by the city fathers for Florence. Although he always considered himself a sculptor rather than a painter, his most famous work remains the frescoes covering the ceiling of the Sistine Chapel in the Vatican, Rome. Michelangelo spent four years lying on his back on a scaffolding to complete this commission for Pope Julius II.

As well as monumental fresco paintings, Renaissance painters produced masterpieces of easel painting, using oil paints introduced from the North. In Venice, the painters Giovanni Bellini (c1430–1516) and Giorgione (c1478–1511) developed a style of painting which used light and colour to convey mood. Titian (c1487–1576) trained in the workshops of both Bellini and Giorgione, and during his long career, he developed a style which ranked with the other great masters of the High Renaissance. He worked directly onto the canvas, using thick brushes, sponges and sometimes his fingers, to achieve

Above *La Pietà, sculpted by Michelangelo in 1498–99 for St Peter's Basilica in Rome. This sculpture, carved during Michelangelo's first visit to Rome, established his reputation. The delicate modelling and high finish show supreme mastery of carving marble, while a difficult composition is cleverly resolved, managing to be at once flowing and rhythmic, yet compact and pyramidal in form.*

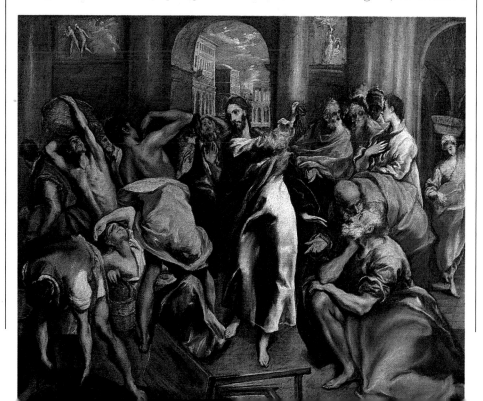

Left Christ Driving the Traders from the Temple *by El Greco, c.1600. In the National Gallery, London. El Greco (the Greek) (1541–1614) was born in Crete and worked in Venice and Rome before settling in Toledo, Spain. Although strongly influenced by Italian painters he developed a highly individual style, distinguished by its bold colouring and elongated forms. El Greco painted this subject several times. Christ's act probably symbolized the Counter-Reformation drive to purge the Catholic Church of heresy.*

Right *Gianlorenzo Bernini was the greatest sculptor of the Baroque period. He created a theatrical illusion using marble, gilded wood and light from a hidden window for this life-size group of* Saint Theresa and the Angel, *in the Cornaro Chapel, Santa Maria della Vittoria, Rome. The sculpture shows an angel piercing the saint's heart with an arrow of love, and is full of drama and emotion.*

rich, glowing colours and capture fleeting effects of light and shadow. Although his handling of the paint could be direct and spontaneous, his paintings nevertheless display the skilful compositions and overall harmony which are typical of works of the High Renaissance.

Baroque art

The style of art produced during the seventeenth century, when painting, sculpture and architecture were often used together to create dramatic illusions, is known as Baroque. The term 'baroque' may come from the Portuguese '*barroco*', for an irregularly-shaped pearl, and suggests the qualities of drama, movement and assymetry which are characteristic of art of the period.

In Catholic countries, Baroque art marks the time of the Counter-Reformation, when the Church authorities, facing the challenge of Protestantism, were anxious to win back the faithful. The greatest sculptor of the Baroque period was Gianlorenzo Bernini (1598–1680).

The same Baroque qualities can be found in the paintings of Peter Paul Rubens (1577–1640) who lived in Flanders. Rubens was born a Protestant but was converted to Roman Catholicism. His paintings use rich, glowing colours, lively, often diagonal compositions and energetic handling of the paint to involve the spectator. This was one of the chief aims of Baroque art.

The Italian painter Caravaggio (1573–1610) involved the spectator by making his life-size works powerfully realistic, using devices such as dramatic foreshortening and piercing shafts of light. Other artists, like the Carracci brothers (painting between c1580 and c1609), created fanciful illusions in fresco paintings covering walls, domes and ceilings. Sometimes it appeared as if paintings were set in elaborate marble surrounds, or that a ceiling was open to the sky. The soaring effects of these vast frescoes are examples of High Baroque, but as the style spread through Europe, it took on other, different forms. In Holland, a Protestant country, the painter Rembrandt van Rijn (1606–69) developed a style of painting which involves the spectator, but on a more intimate, personal level. He used dramatic *chiaroscuro*, flooding his canvases with deep, velvety shadows, to create a powerful, sometimes mystical mood.

Left *Rembrandt's* Woman Bathing in a Stream, *painted 1654–55. In the National Gallery, London. The Model is believed to be Hendrickje Stoffels, who became Rembrandt's mistress from about 1649.*

Rococo art

In the early eighteenth century, a new style affecting painting, sculpture and architecture emerged in Europe – the Rococo. The term means 'shell-like' and describes the decorative, delicate style of painting and sculpture which fitted well into the elegant, fussy interiors of the time. Artists painted scenes from Classical mythology or history in soft, pastel colours and theatrical, stage-like settings. Their works reflected the elegance and playfulness of life at the French court, and François Boucher (1703–70), whose works are typical of the French Rococo style, became the favourite painter of Madame de Pompadour, mistress of King Louis XV.

Neoclassicism

The Oath of the Horatii, painted by the French artist Jacques Louis David (1748–1825), heralded a new style, Neoclassicism. Neoclassical art was both a reaction against the frivolity of the Rococo, and a new response to Classical Antiquity, following the excavations of the cities of Pompeii and Herculaneum in 1748. Rococo artists had chosen playful scenes from Classical mythology. Now David chose a solemn subject from Roman history, the moment when the three Horatii brothers swear to their father that they will fight to the death against the brothers from Alba, for the sake of Rome. The painting is severely simple and carefully composed, in keeping with its message of moral courage. Five years after David painted *The Oath*, the French Revolution overthrew King Louis XVI, and established the first French Republic. David became the official painter of the Revolution. The severe simplicity of his paintings is echoed in the smooth, carved marble sculptures of the Italian Antonio Canova (1757–1822).

Above The Oath of the Horatii *by Jacques Louis David, painted in 1784. It is in the Musée du Louvre, Paris.*

Romantic art

Neoclassical artists looked to Classical history for their subjects. Theodore Géricault (1791–1824) had sketched soldiers in action on the battlefield during the Napoleonic Wars, and his paintings seek romance in real life – expressing a new spirit in art – the spirit of Romanticism. In 1819 Géricault completed a massive painting, the *Raft of the Medusa*, depicting the shipwrecked survivors of a French frigate which had sunk off the coast of Senegal in 1816. Géricault worked with painstaking fidelity to his subject. He made drawings and sketches of corpses in a Paris morgue, and asked the ship's carpenter to make a model of the raft. After Géricault died following a horse-riding accident at the age of thirty-three, Eugène Delacroix (1798–1863) became the leading Romantic painter. He chose themes of man fighting against nature, such as the excitement of an Arabian tiger hunt, and used swirling forms and thick paint in a lively manner to express his feelings and emotions as he painted. Romantic painters and sculptors believed that the artist's feelings were as important as his subject. In their belief in their own creative freedom, they were the first modern artists.

⑥ The Modern Age

Left *Monet's view of the port of Le Havre, exhibited in Paris in 1874 under the title* Impression: Sunrise *earned the Impressionists their name. Critics attacked Monet's broad, sketchy use of paint and lack of surface 'finish', dismissing such paintings as mere 'impressions' or sketches.*

Below Mme Leroy Washing *by Mary Cassatt (1845–1926). Cassatt was an American-born artist who moved to Paris and became associated with the Impressionists. Her subjects, often intimate domestic scenes, show a fine sense of colour and design, influenced by Japanese woodblock prints.*

The nineteenth century brought the Machine Age. Science was advancing fast, with new inventions in every field, from industry and transport to photography. Many people moved to the cities to find work, and industrialization brought wealth to some and poverty to others. In the art world, the middle classes, prosperous through manufacture and trade, became the new patrons, and art was now available to a wider public through annual exhibitions held in cities like London and Paris.

Subjects from the Classical past seemed to have less and less relevance to modern life, and with the works of Gustave Courbet (1819–77) a new movement, Realism, was established. Courbet painted everyday scenes of peasant life on a grand scale, using broad, bold brushwork. His paintings seemed crude and ugly to many when they were first exhibited.

In the cafés of Paris, a group of young artists including Édouard Manet (1832–83), Claude Monet (1840–1926), Pierre Auguste Renoir (1841–1919) and Camille Pissarro (1830–1903), began meeting to exchange ideas. The Impressionists, as they came to be known, believed that an artist should paint what he saw. They were interested

Above Cypresses and Two Figures *by Vincent Van Gogh. During his stay at the mental asylum at St Rémy in the south of France, Van Gogh spent many days out sketching in the countryside. This was one of the last landscapes he painted there and shows the style he had evolved. Thick, clotted paint and dynamic, spiralling brushwork are used to bring the trees and the night sky to life.*

in learning from the new art of photography, and from scientific theories about light and colour. They learnt, for example, that shadows are never black, but are always tinged with colour, and they began to paint using small dabs of pure colour on a white canvas. They painted out of doors, capturing their impressions of the landscape and scenes from everyday life. To contemporaries, their techniques appeared hurried and sketchy.

Just as the Impressionists were rethinking painting, the sculptor Auguste Rodin (1840–1917), was rethinking sculpture. Like the Impressionists, he ignored demands for a smooth surface 'finish'. His stone sculptures sometimes appear as if they are just struggling out of the block, while his bronzes, cast from clay or plaster models, retain the energetic modelling and lively play of light and shade that he created by shaping his materials directly with his hands. Rodin worked from the living model where he could, often trying to capture the sudden gestures and movements of models moving or relaxing about his studio.

Other painters followed the lead of the Impressionists in working directly in fresh colours on a white ground. Paul Cézanne (1839–1906) looked to the underlying structure, or skeleton, of nature which he saw in geometric terms as the cylinder, the sphere and the cone, building his images with overlapping blocks of colour.

In the works of Post-Impressionists such as Cézanne, Paul Gauguin (1848–1903) and Vincent Van Gogh (1853–90), forms and colours are simplified, with the artist drawing on various influences such as Japanese prints and Polynesian sculpture. Painters were now making bold and free use of strong colours for their own sake and not just because they corresponded to the objects represented. In France, a group of young painters led by Henri Matisse (1869–1954) used colour so daringly that they were nicknamed *Les Fauves* (wild beasts). They painted purple skies, red trees and orange water, ignoring traditional concerns such as three-dimensional form and perspective in favour of strong statements of colour and pattern.

Artists were no longer content to paint pictures *of* the world. They wanted to paint pictures *about* the world, and the way they saw it. Van Gogh had used swirling brush strokes and vivid colours to express his

Right By the Sea, *sculpted in marble by Auguste Rodin.*

troubled emotions. In the twentieth century, 'Expressionist' artists like Edvard Munch (1863–1944), Emil Nolde (1867–1956) and Max Beckmann (1884–1950) conveyed a sense of loneliness and despair following the First World War (1914–18) through harsh colours and distorted forms.

Above *Gaugin was born in Paris but spent the later years of his life in Tahiti, where he developed a highly decorative style of painting, using rich colours. In Pastorales Tahitiennes, painted in 1893, he used pure green and vermilion, which he said reminded him of old Dutch paintings or an old tapestry. He wanted to convey the simplicity of the native life through art which was free of naturalistic conventions.*

Left The Scream *by the Norwegian artist Edvard Munch, painted in 1893. In the National Gallery, Oslo. In his diaries, Munch wrote that he wanted to stop painting 'interiors and women knitting'. Here, he uses expressionist devices such as harsh colours and disturbing, swirling lines, to make the scream almost 'visible'.*

33

Above Woman Weeping *by Pablo Picasso, painted in 1937. In this painting Picasso uses strident colours and agitated, fragmented forms to convey the woman's inner torment.*

Below Parade Amoureuse *by the Dadaist painter Francis Picabia. In one of a series of 'ironical machines' painted between 1915–1924, Picabia uses the shapes and rhythms of machine parts to suggest mechanical movement.*

The Cubist movement was equally ambitious. Cubism was developed in the early years of this century by the Spanish artist Pablo Picasso (1881–1973) and the French painter Georges Braque (1882–1963). Like Cézanne, the Cubists looked for the underlying structure, but they went further, examining their subjects from all angles at once, breaking them up and rearranging them on the canvas like jigsaw pieces. Inspired by early Iberian sculpture and African Negro carvings, Picasso simplified forms into overlapping angular shapes. Later, he and Braque experimented with collage, using sand mixed with oil paints, and faking textures like wood and marble. In sculpture too, Picasso introduced new materials and techniques, using the parts of a bicycle to suggest a bull's head, for example.

In contrast, a group of artists in Italy, led by the writer Marinetti, celebrated the machine age; of motor cars, skyscrapers, trains and cities. These 'Futurist' artists like Umberto Boccioni (1882–1916) and Gino Severini (1800–1900) wanted their works to capture the energy and progress of the modern world. In his sculpture, Boccioni attempted to represent the different stages of action in a single figure.

The same use of 'found objects' inspired another movement – Dada (a nonsense name meaning hobbyhorse in French). The Dadaists attacked the modern age, in particular the values of society which caused the madness and wastage of the 1914–18 World War. They were rebelling against the art of the past, which they saw as representing the old world order that had failed. Marcel Duchamp (1887–1968) expressed this rebellion when he put a moustache and beard on a reproduction of Leonardo's *Mona Lisa*, and began to exhibit 'ready-mades'. By signing and exhibiting such objects as art, he was suggesting that people now valued names more than art itself. Francis Picabia (1879–1953) mocked modern machines by painting useless objects like 'an instrument that could measure the loneliness of the sun'. Dada soon became an international movement with groups in Europe and America. Wherever they were, Dadaists caused outrage by staging wild exhibitions where, for example, viewers would be given axes and asked to chop the exhibits up!

After the First World War artists and writers gathered around the poet André Breton in Paris and founded the Surrealist movement. Influenced by the shock tactics of Dada and the theories of Sigmund Freud, they sought to use the subconscious to produce images which could express the true nature of thought, as they saw it. (Freud believed that a person's 'subconscious' is made up of memories, desires and fears which are usually hidden, but which can and do affect thoughts and behaviour without the person realizing it.)

Surrealism took many different forms, from the light, airy visions of Joan Miró (b1893) to the strange, nightmarish landscapes of Salvador Dali (1904–89), in which nothing seems solid, and one object melts into another. Surrealist painters, such as Max Ernst (1891–1976), used 'automatic drawing' (making marks, shapes and patterns automatically and without thought) to suggest ideas for images.

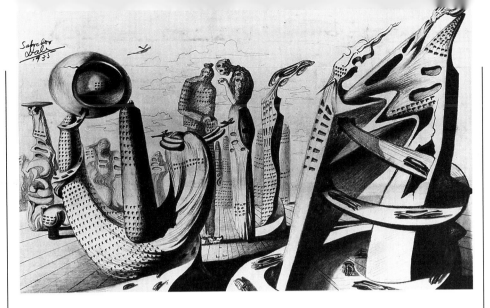

Artists from the Renaissance onwards had tried to represent reality: their art was representational or figurative, showing figures realistically in space. Now, they were more concerned with communicating their own feelings. In order to do this, some began to simplify and 'abstract', working with pure colours, lines and shapes to express their mood or feelings. The first painter to explore this new approach was the Russian Wassily Kandinsky (1866–1944). Another Russian, Kasimir Malevich (1878–1935) simplified still further, using only geometric shapes, while the Dutch painter Piet Mondrian (1872–1944) worked with 'grid' patterns and the primary colours red, yellow and blue, with black and white.

In sculpture, Barbara Hepworth (1903–75) used abstract forms to suggest rocks, foliage or landscape. Henry Moore (1898–1986) transformed the human form into massive, monumental shapes in wood, bronze or stone. His works were influenced by unsophisticated and ancient cultures, especially those of West Africa and Pre-Columbian Mexico. Their rounded volumes and open, air-filled spaces remind us of caves and rocks worn away by water.

Abstract art was one of the influences on a new school of painting which grew up in the USA between the First and Second World Wars. After the outbreak of the Second World War (1939–45), many artists fled Europe to settle in the USA, bringing with them different ideas drawn from Expressionism, Cubism, Surrealism and Abstraction, which all gave rise to Abstract Expressionism. In the mid 1940s, the American-born painter Jackson Pollock (1912–56) developed a method of Action or Drip painting, in which he worked on large canvases laid on the floor, flicking paint from sticks to produce pictures made up of interwoven patterns of drips which corresponded to his movements while painting. In this, he was following methods similar to those used by the early native American Indians in their sand pictures. Pollock worked with ordinary domestic paints often on vast canvases, designed to surround the spectator and involve him or her in the action. Museums and galleries specializing in modern art were beginning to commission works directly from artists, and the enormous scale of Pollock's works reflected this trend.

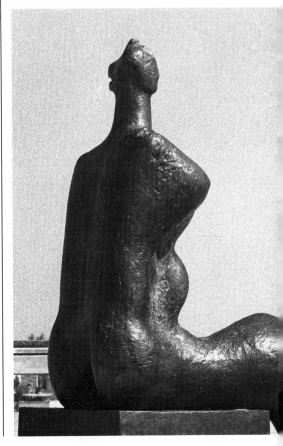

A very different interpretation of Abstract Expressionism is shown in the works of Mark Rothko (1903–1970), in which colour appears to float, almost as if it is about to dissolve, and simple shapes and colour combinations create the mood and convey the artist's feelings.

The Abstract Expressionists wanted to explore the internal world of their own minds or subconscious. Pop artists, whose work emerged in London and New York in the 1950s, wanted to explore the external world of 'popular culture': comics, advertisements, packaging, television and film. Artists like David Hockney (b1937) and Andy Warhol (1931–1987) used bright colours and techniques such as silk screen printing for mass reproduction of their images. Another post-war movement, Op art, aimed to create the illusion of movement in a painting through optical effects of colour, shape and pattern.

During the second half of the twentieth century, there has been an increasing variety of styles and movements existing together, overlapping and developing from one another. New ideas and revivals of earlier styles co-exist, but the underlying trend has been away from the well-crafted art object and towards 'conceptual art', expressing the artist's ideas through a variety of means. The artist might use his or her own or a model's body, or the landscape itself to express ideas, while video and graffiti have become new art forms in their own right. All sorts of materials are used, from 'found objects', lasers and holograms to photographs. Media are often mixed, and sculpture and painting are much less clearly defined activities. The bewildering range of art forms existing today is a reflection of our rapidly changing lifestyles, in an age dominated by the technology explosion and the mass media.

Left Afternoon Swimming *by the English artist David Hockney. This lithograph in colours was executed in 1979.*

Painting

The painter's materials are called 'media' and include oil, watercolour, acrylic and vinyl paints, coloured chalks, and ink. These media are applied to a 'support', such as canvas, wood panel, paper, glass or silk, using a variety of tools – brushes, fingers, palette knife, sponges or air brushes. Below the surface of a painting, there may be other layers of paint, usually called under-painting, and often there is a 'ground' which helps the paint to stick to the support without soaking into it and becoming weakened. According to the artist's use or handling of materials, such as the size of the brush, the direction of brushstrokes, and the underlayers of paint, different effects can be created.

Oil paints were first used successfully by the brothers Jan and Hubert van Eyck who worked in Flanders (now in Belgium) in the early fifteenth century. Before that time, artists had worked chiefly with tempera (usually pigment mixed with egg and thinned with water) for small-scale works and for the fresco method of wall painting. In true fresco painting (*buon fresco*) such as Michelangelo's

Below *A painter working in oil paints.*

Sistine Chapel frescoes, tempera is applied to fresh, damp plaster (fresco is Italian for fresh) which absorbs and binds the pigments as they dry. Colours are typically pale, earth colours, (they must be resistant to the lime in the plaster), and the medium dries quickly, forcing the artist to work swiftly. Shading is indicated by short cross strokes or 'hatching' in a darker colour. The use of fresco declined after the sixteenth century, when oil and canvas provided a more versatile and convenient method of painting. Even large canvases, may be rolled for transport.

Oil paints, used on canvas or board, have been the chief medium of painting in the West for over 400 years. Oils can be thick or fluid and are slow-drying, allowing the painter to work slowly, blending colours and even scraping or wiping the paint off and reworking as he or she wishes. Opaque areas may be contrasted with thin, transparent glazes which alter the colour of the layer beneath, as coloured glass would do.

The colour of the ground on which the artist works is an important factor. Early oil painters, such as the van Eycks, used a white 'gesso' ground to give their colours brilliance. Then, in the late sixteenth century, Venetian painters began using a coloured ground, often a reddish-brown, to give overall warmth and harmony. Painters continued to work on coloured grounds until the nineteenth century, when the Impressionists, seeking to capture outdoor light and freshness, returned to using a white-primed canvas. They often used a technique called *alla prima*, working directly onto the ground rather than building up the paint surface in successive layers. Portable materials, such as commercial paints in soft, metal tubes, were now available and scientific research had introduced new and brighter permanent pigments such as cobalt blue.

During the twentieth century, artists have experimented with mixed media. For example, oil paints are combined with tar, gravel, sand or mud to create rich surface textures. The freedom of modern artists to work experimentally has been increased by technological advances such as the introduction of vinyl and acrylic paints (pigments bound with synthetic plastic resin) producing clear, bright colours which dry quickly.

Other artists have continued to work in traditional media such as watercolour. Watercolour is finely powdered pigment bound with gum and then thinned with water. Many artists have used watercolour for outdoor sketching as it is a convenient, portable medium. Traditionally, watercolour is laid onto paper or card in transparent washes, working from the lightest tone to the darkest. The white paper will reflect through, giving a fresh, sparkling quality. The painter can add highlights by scratching away the surface or leaving patches bare, or by using opaque white 'bodycolour' or gouache. Poster paints or designers' colour are a form of gouache. Artists such as Picasso and Kandinsky used gouache for its rich effects and rapid-drying qualities. Gouache is also the medium used in Indian, Persian and Turkish miniature painting.

Above Irises, *by David Armitage. Watercolours are both fluid and transparent, and here the artist has exploited these qualities, using a free, wet handling and allowing the colours to run and overlap.*

Collage and assemblage

Twentieth-century artists have also experimented with collage, that is building up pictures by gluing materials such as paper and cloth onto the support. Interesting surface effects can be included by using frottage, the method of rubbing impressions from a textured surface (like making a coin or brass rubbing). Montage uses photographs or printed material, like the newspaper clippings stuck onto canvas by the Cubist painters Picasso and Braque.

Assemblage assembles materials in the same way as collage, but in three-dimensions. All kinds of materials may be glued, welded, tied or pinned together. Assemblage is one of the ways in which twentieth century artists have broken down traditional barriers between painting and sculpture.

Sculpture

Today, the term sculpture covers a wide range of art forms and materials, but the sculptor's work falls into four main categories: modelling, casting, carving and construction.

Modelling is a very direct method of sculpture because the sculptor works chiefly with the hands, shaping a soft material such as clay, wax, plaster or papier mâché. Shaped wooden tools, knives or wire loops may also be used. The marks or impressions left by the fingers or tools may be used to give surface texture, or the sculptor may choose to smooth out all traces of handling. For larger modelled sculptures, an armature (see diagram right) of metal and wood may be used to give strength.

The materials used for modelling allow the sculptor to experiment with projecting forms, lively compositions and surface textures. These qualities can be retained if the wax or plaster model is then cast in a metal such as bronze or aluminium. Clay can also be set hard by firing in a kiln. Sculpture in fired clay is often called terracotta (baked earth). Once fired, the terracotta can be glazed or decorated with coloured slips (liquid clay), and these may be set hard by re-firing.

The metal traditionally used for *casting* sculpture is bronze, an alloy made mainly of copper and tin, but metals such as lead and aluminium may also be used. One method of casting in metal is to make a wax model which is then surrounded by clay, plaster or sand. The mould is baked, melting out the wax and leaving a 'negative impression' of the work, which can then be filled with molten metal. Casts can also be made in plaster, plastics, clay slip (which has to be fired), wax, and even papier mâché.

Many twentieth-century sculptors, including Pablo Picasso and Eduardo Paolozzi, have used casting to create clever, often comical works from assemblages, as in Picasso's *Baboon and Young*, which uses a toy car for the head and a pot for the body.

Carving involves cutting or drilling materials such as bone, stone and wood. Stone sculpture needs careful planning and control. The sculptor, working from preliminary drawings, will block out the rough

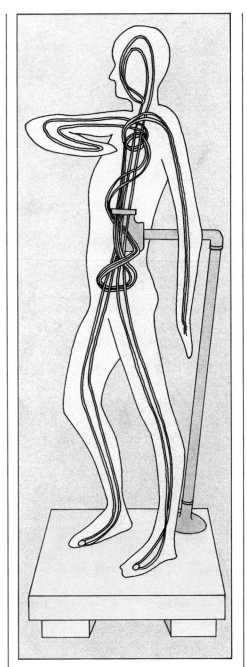

Above *Diagram of an armature.*

Left *The English sculptress Barbara Hepworth (1903–1975) carving in wood. She experimented ceaselessly with hollowed-out, open forms, sometimes painting the insides white, or using strings as if in a musical instrument, which she said represented 'the tension I feel between myself, the sea, the wind and the hills.'*

form using a metal hammer. A wooden mallet is then used with the finer finishing tools. Stone is heavy and hard and lacks 'tensile' strength, which means that the sculptor must avoid fragile projections (such as an extended arm or leg) and unsupported shapes. Before power tools were invented, all stone carving was done either with a hammer and chisel, or by pounding and abrading (scraping away). In cultures which lacked metal tools, hard stone was carved by wearing away the surface through pounding it to a powder then rubbing it with a hard abrasive such as emery.

The fibrous nature of wood gives it great strength along its grain. As long as the sculptor follows the grain, the wood can be carved into thin and extended shapes, and treated more freely than stone. The nature of wood varies widely. Pine, for example, is soft with an uneven

Left *A sculptor working with clay.*

grain. Boxwood is hard and dense with no clear grain. Boxwood carvings must be small, because of the size of the tree, while those in pine can reach the size of the North American totem pole.

Wood can also be used in the form of boards, blocks, logs, and can even be moulded by wetting it whilst it is under pressure. The sculptor may join blocks or slabs, and can either bring out the colour and grain by polishing, or may paint or otherwise decorate the surface of the sculpture.

Construction is the art of building up a sculpture by putting together various component parts. Modern industrial technology has made available a wide range of new materials and processes. The sculptor uses materials such as plywood, plastics, glass, metal, perspex, pipes, girders, ropes and wire. These may be bolted, screwed, glued or welded together, or moulded to create shapes in space.

Actual motion, natural or mechanical, may also be used, as in Alexander Calder's mobiles, which are designed to move with the air currents. 'Light' sculptures have also been made, using, for example, specially shaped electrical strip lighting. Objects or parts of objects used in construction are chosen for the way they look or the associations they carry. Pop artists have made us look again at familiar objects such as Cola cans or Oxo boxes, by presenting them in unexpected settings or on an unusual scale.

Print-making

The various methods of print-making have become popular art forms in their own right today. There are four main print-making processes: relief, intaglio, lithography and screen-printing.

Relief printing involves the cutting away of some surface areas from a wood or lino block, leaving raised areas to be inked with a roller and then pressed onto paper. The cut-away parts will remain white, while the inked 'relief' parts will print onto paper. Potato printing is a simple form of relief printing, but sharp tools are needed to cut away the wood or lino. Japanese prints use a number of wood-cut blocks, one for each colour printed.

The *intaglio* process uses a metal plate (usually copper or zinc) into which designs are either cut with a tool or 'etched' away by acid. Ink is rubbed over the plate, and into the cut lines or channels. Then the ink is cleaned off the surface of the plate before a sheet of dampened paper is pressed onto the plate, picking up the ink from the grooves. Dry-point, line engraving, etching, mezzotint and aquatint are all forms of intaglio printing.

Lithography is a kind of printing where a surface, of stone or metal, is thoroughly cleaned before the image is drawn or painted on using an oily crayon or liquid. Next the surface is made wet, although the water runs off the areas that were drawn upon. Then oil-based ink is rolled over the surface; the wet areas resist the oily ink, while it is attracted to the areas made greasy by the drawing. Lastly, paper is pressed onto the surface and picks up the ink clinging to the drawn areas and so transferring the image. 'Offset' lithography involves another stage, where the image is transferred from the surface to a large roller which then lays the ink down onto the paper. This has the advantage of printing the image the way it was drawn, whereas direct lithography (like relief and intaglio) prints the reverse of the drawn image. Newspapers and posters are usually printed by offset machines.

Screen-printing is a process using a mesh screen, made of silk (serigraphy) or synthetic material, which has a weave open enough to allow ink to be pushed through it. The material is stretched over a frame so that it is evenly taut, then the negative of the image to be printed is masked out by one of various means: placing a stencil such as cut-out paper on top of the paper to be printed on before the screen is placed on top of it; using a stick-on stencil which is attached to the screen itself; using a masking fluid which blocks the mesh and can be painted directly onto the screen and allowed to dry. The screen is then placed onto the paper, ink put onto the back of the screen and dragged across it with a squeegee (a tool with a thick, straight-edged piece of rubber set into a handle) which forces the ink through the mesh and onto the paper. The stencil prevents the ink reaching the paper in the negative parts of the image, so only the positive is printed.

Photographic images can be transferred onto screens and lithographic plates using a process called 'half tone', which converts the image into a series of small dots, as can be seen on black and white newspaper photographs. Andy Warhol's *Marilyn* is an example of a screen-printed photographic image.

Below *Silk screen printing.*

Further Information

Books about art can introduce you to an artist's works, or to a style of painting, but it is important to try to see a painting or sculpture at first hand, whenever possible. By looking at a reproduction of a work of art in a book, you cannot get a true sense of the size of the work or the artist's handling. There is not enough space to list all the world's major art galleries – the following lists some of the world's most important art collections. Other places to see works of art include commercial art galleries and auction houses, where exhibitions are constantly changing.

Britain
British Museum, London. Ancient art including African, Oceanic, Egyptian, Classical and Far Eastern.
National Gallery, London. Italian and Northern masters: English collection.
Tate Gallery, London. British and modern collections: Turner Collection.
Victoria and Albert Museum, London. Collections of decorative and fine arts dating from early Christian times to the present. Special collections from the Middle and Far East, and India.
Burrell Collection, Glasgow. Nineteenth-century French paintings: collections of textiles, ceramics, stained glass.

Australia
National Gallery of Victoria, Melbourne. Collection of European Masters.
Art Gallery of New South Wales, Sydney. Historical collection: contemporary Australian art; Aboriginal art.

Austria
Kunsthistorisches Museum, Vienna. European art from Renaissance to late nineteenth century.

Egypt
Egyptian Museum, Cairo. Egyptian art from prehistory to Roman times.

France
Musee du Louvre, Paris. National collection from Egyptian to Pre-Impressionists.
Musée D'Orsay, Paris. Nineteenth century art including Impressionist collection.
Centre National d'art et de culture Georges Pompidou, National collection of modern art.

Italy
Uffizi Gallery, Florence. Italian and Northern Renaissance masters.

Japan
National Museum, Tokyo. Japanese art; Chinese art.

Mexico
National Museum of Anthropology, Mexico City. Pre-Hispanic Mexican art.

Netherlands
Rijksmuseum, Amsterdam. Dutch art from fifteenth to nineteenth century.

Spain
Prado, Madrid. Master paintings from fifteenth to eighteenth century including Spanish collection.

United States
Metropolitan Museum, New York. Egyptian to modern art collections.
Museum of Modern Art, New York. Comprehensive collection of modern art.

USSR
Hermitage, Leningrad Extensive collections from medieval to the twentieth century.
Pushkin Museum, Moscow. Nineteenth and twentieth century collections.

Career Information

Only the exceptionally talented and lucky can make a living purely from the practice of painting or sculpture. Some artists make a living by teaching or by working with regional arts associations or community arts projects. There are, however, a number of career options open to those interested in painting and sculpture. The following list indicates broad areas of interest.

Arts administration/Curatorial work in museum and gallery collections, commercial art galleries
Art teaching in schools, colleges, educational departments within a museum or gallery.

Community arts leisure activities, projects with regional arts associations; further education.
Art therapy in schools, hospitals, clinics, prisons, day centres.
Art history and criticism Writing books for newspapers, magazines, radio and television.
Conservation and Restoration in museums and galleries, commercial restoration firms, craft workshops, private collections.
Design and illustration in the fields of advertising, industry or publishing. Includes graphic design (display, lettering, packaging) and three-dimensional design (industrial, product, interior, theatre).

Further Reading

Dictionary of Art and Artists by PETER AND LINDA MURRAY. (Penguin, 1988)
Looking at Art – A History of Painting and Sculpture by NORBERT LYNTON (Kingfisher, 1981)
The Story of Art by ERNST H. GOMBRICH (Phaidon, 1984)
Techniques of the World's Great Painters ed. WALDEMAR JANUSZCZAK (New Burlington Books, Phaidon,1988)
Understanding Art by WALDEMAR JANUSZCZAK and JENNY McCLEERY (Macdonald, 1982)
Ways of Seeing by JOHN BERGER (BBC/Penguin, 1972)
Women Artists by KAREN PETERSEN and J.J. WILSON (The Women's Press, 1978)

Glossary

Abstract Usually refers to an image or form which does not represent anything else. Also the activity of *taking* a form, shape, or pattern *from* the appearance of something.

Amphora A Greek or Roman two-handled vessel.

Armature A support structure which remains hidden inside a sculpture, like a skeleton, mostly made of metal or wood.

Bronze A mixture of copper and tin, which when heated until it melts can be used for casting. Also an object cast in bronze.

Cast The activity of creating an object by pouring a liquid which sets hard (such as bronze, plaster, plastic resin) into a 'mould', which is the negative shape of the object to be cast. Also the object thus created.

Chiaroscuro Italian for 'light-dark', meaning the use of light and shade in a painting.

Collage A composition made from pieces of paper, cloth, photographs and other materials pasted onto a dry ground.

Composition The organization of shapes, colours and areas of light and dark in a painting.

Dark Ages The period between about the fifth to tenth centuries, considered to be an unenlightened period in Europe.

Easel painting Painting pictures of a size, and in a medium, suitable for working upon an easel (as opposed to murals and icons).

Foreshortening The use of the laws of perspective, applied to a single figure or object.

Form A three-dimensional shape, or its representation in two dimensions.

Found object A man-made or natural object, found and used, unaltered, in a work of art, either by itself or with other objects.

Fresco The technique of painting onto plaster, on walls and ceilings.

Gesso A 'ground' made from glue and white powder. It has the qualities of being very white, fairly hard, brittle and absorbent; used especially on wooden panels and for tempera painting.

Gilding Covering with gold. In painting and sculpture this has often been done using gold 'leaf', an extremely thin gold foil, which is glued or rubbed on.

Glaze A thin layer of transparent or translucent paint which allows the colour beneath to show through. Also the glassy coating 'fired' onto ceramics.

Gouache A 'watercolour' paint with white pigment added, making the colours more opaque.

Grid A pattern of straight lines, set at right angles, usually regular and spaced equally.

Ground A substance applied to a 'support', before painting begins, which helps the paint to adhere to the support without damaging it and without it becoming weakened.

Handling The way an artist responds to and uses materials, derived from the way an artist literally handles clay, paint etc.

Hatching Short, parallel strokes used to achieve the effect of shading, especially in drawing, printing and tempera.

Hologram Patterns produced by light beams.

Illumination Decorating written texts in books.

Laser A device for generating intense beams of light.

Medium (Plural – media) In painting and sculpture, the materials an artist uses to make a piece of art. Usually a 'medium' is a recognized set of materials and techniques, such as oil painting on canvas, or casting in bronze.

Mosaic A picture made by cementing little cubes (tesserae) of coloured material (traditionally glass or stone) together to make an image or pattern. Mostly made directly on walls, ceilings or floors.

Mural Painting on walls; implies very large scale, to fill the wall.

Patron Someone who supports an artist by commissioning and/or buying work. Patronage may come from an individual, a trades guild or company, a church or the state.

Perspective The method of showing three-dimensional figures or objects, usually on a flat surface, to make it appear that they have depth and occupy space.

Pigment Coloured material which gives paint its colour, usually ground into a fine powder and mixed with a binder, which holds it together and makes it stick to the support.

Pre-Columbian Relating to the Americas before the arrival of Columbus, in the fifteenth century.

Relief sculpture Sculpture which is carved into a surface, and so is not free-standing or 'in-the-round'.

Sfumato Italian word, originally from the word for 'smoke', describing the gradual merging of colour or 'tone', with no sudden changes.

Shading The illusion of shadow created by the use of dark tone or colour.

Support The material or structure, such as canvas, paper or wood, onto which paint is applied to make a painting.

Tempera Paint using egg as the binder, usually yolk but sometimes the white or whole egg. Soluble in water before drying.

Tone The darkness or lightness of a colour. Also used to describe the shades of grey between (and including) black and white.

Totem A representation of a natural object or animal, adopted by North American Indians as an emblem.

Underpainting Layers of paint beneath the top layer of a painting, particularly those which show through 'glazes' or semi-transparent top layers.

Picture acknowledgements

Bridgemen Art Library cover, 4 (top), 6 (lower), 17, 18 (lower), 19, 21, 22 (lower), 23 (lower), 24 (both), 25, 26 (lower), 27, 28, 29, 30 (both), 31 (top), 32 (lower), 33, 34 (both), 36; David Cumming 7, 37, 38; Julia Davey 41, 42; Chris Fairclough 15 (lower); Marion and Tony Morrison 15 (top); Ann Ronan 22 (top); Ronald Sheridan 4 (lower), 5, 8, 9, 10 (both), 11, 12 (both), 13, 14, 18 (top), 20 (top), 23 (top), 35 (lower); Topham Picture Library 32 (top), 40 (top); Wayland Picture Library 6 (upper), 16, 20 (lower), 26 (top), 31 (lower), 35 (top). Diagram on page 39 by Malcolm Walker.
Works by the following artists appear by courtesy of: Dali © DEMART PRO ARTE BV 1989; Picabia © ADAGP, Paris, DACS, London, 1989; Picasso © DACS 1989.

Index